ROYAL SUTTON COLDFIELD
T O W N   C O U N C I L

Funded by Royal Sutton Coldfield
Town Council's Community Grant Programme

Mapping

by Nancy Harris

raintree 🍃

a Capstone company — publishers for children

a Capstone company — publishers for children

Raintree is an imprint of Capstone Global Library Limited,
a company incorporated in England and Wales having its registered office at
264 Banbury Road, Oxford, OX2 7DY – Registered company number: 6695582

www.raintree.co.uk

Image credits
Alamy: jackie ellis, 10, Kevin Wheal, 15, Mark Gibson, 16; Capstone: Eric Gohl, 29, Capstone: HL
Studios, 11, 18 Bottom, 20, 21, 22, 25, 26; Dreamstime: Leremy, 19; Newscom: Andre Jenny Stock
Connection Worldwide, 6 Bottom, Jan-Peter Kasper, 5; Shutterstock: Alexey Boldin, 7 Bottom, Alfonso
de Tomas, 24, AridOcean, 9, AVAVA, Cover Bottom, Bardocz Peter, 14, 23, Dragon Images, 31,
Hamik, 13 Bottom, iconspor, Cover Back, Juli Hansen, 1, Design Elements, Merydolia, Cover Top Left,
okili77, 8 Top, 17, parinyabinsuk, 30, Peter Hermes Furian, 13 Top, Peteri, 27, pisaphotography, 7
Top, rzymuR, 8 Bottom, shadowalice, 18 Top, Triff, 12, Vadim Georgiev, Cover Top Right, viphotos, 4,
wavebreakmedia, 6 Top, 7 Middle; Wikimedia: US Army Corps of Engineers, 28

Printed and bound in India.

ISBN: 978 1 4747 9265 3

Contents

Mapping

Throughout history, people have used maps to show what the Earth looks like. Maps are used to show the Earth's land, oceans and waterways. Maps also show the **location** of countries, states and cities in the world.

When learning about communities in the world, people want to know how they can travel from place to place, on roads and motorways. They want to know what the climate, or weather, is like in areas around the world. Mapmakers have been making maps for thousands of years to provide people with this information.

FACT

One of the world's oldest-known maps is about 3,500 years old. It shows a very old city in what is now the country of Iraq. It was cut into a clay tablet.

Map forms

Today maps come in many forms and sizes. People have a number of choices when picking a map that best meets their needs.

Globes

Some maps, such as world maps, can be printed on globes. Globes are often made of metal or plastic and are round like the

Earth. Globes can be large or small. They are examples of what Earth looks like from space.

FACT The world's largest turning globe, called Eartha, is located in the state of Maine, USA. It weighs about 2,540 kilograms (5,600 pounds).

Paper maps

Other maps are printed on paper. There are one-page paper maps, folded paper maps and books of maps, such as books of **road maps**. Some paper maps can be easily carried around, while others are hung up. Paper maps can often be found on classroom walls.

Electronic maps

There are also electronic maps. Electronic maps are shown on computer screens. People can use them on mobile phones, tablets and in cars. Roads and buildings can be seen on some electronic maps. Drivers use them to get directions to a certain place. Some electronic maps let drivers know when roads are closed or very busy. These maps can show drivers how to take other roads to get to where they are going.

Map types

Maps don't all show the same type of information. Just like there are many map forms, there are also many map types.

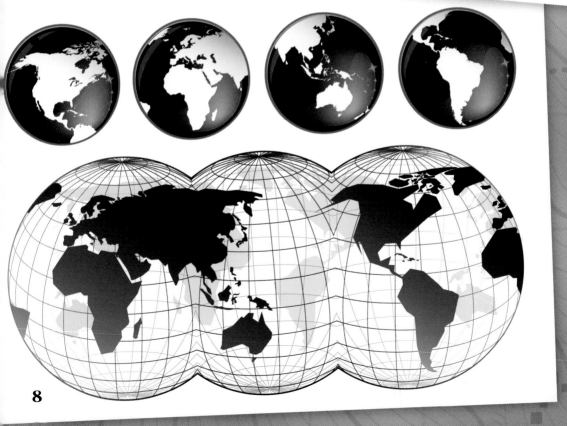

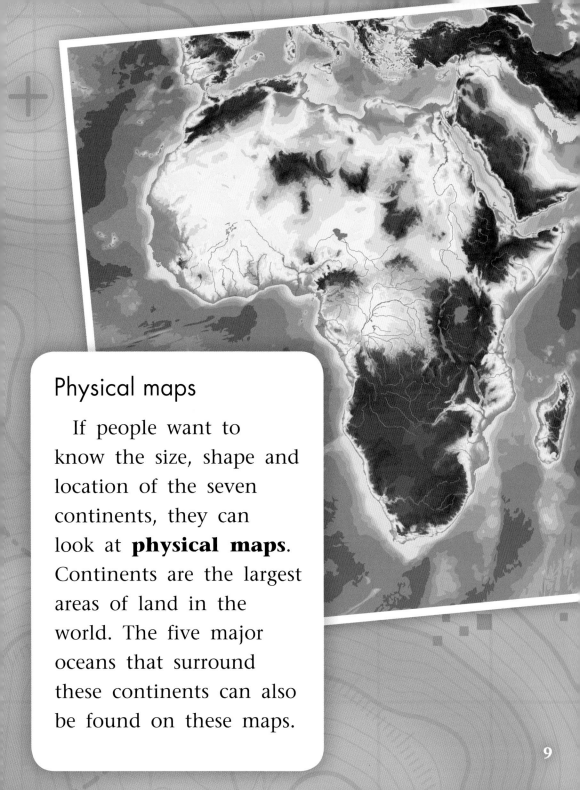

Physical maps

If people want to know the size, shape and location of the seven continents, they can look at **physical maps**. Continents are the largest areas of land in the world. The five major oceans that surround these continents can also be found on these maps.

Physical maps help people learn where landforms, such as mountains and lakes, are located. People also use these types of maps to plan adventures. When planning a hike, a physical map can show the best trails to follow.

Climate maps

Sometimes people want to know what the temperature is like in an area during a certain time of year. They might also want to know how much rain or snow falls there at that time of year. **Climate maps** provide this information.

People use climate maps to learn what it is like to live in different areas of the world. They also use them to plan when and where to go on a trip. For example, climate maps can show the best times to visit a place if you want to avoid rain.

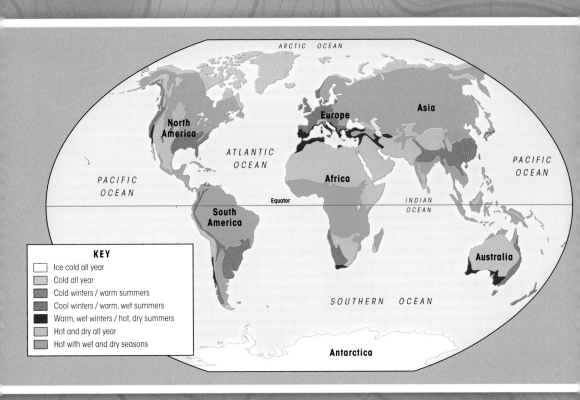

ARCTIC OCEAN

Europe

Asia

North America

ATLANTIC OCEAN

PACIFIC OCEAN

Africa

PACIFIC OCEAN

Equator

INDIAN OCEAN

South America

Australia

KEY
- Ice cold all year
- Cold all year
- Cold winters / warm summers
- Cool winters / warm, wet summers
- Warm, wet winters / hot, dry summers
- Hot and dry all year
- Hot with wet and dry seasons

SOUTHERN OCEAN

Antarctica

Historical maps

Maps are also helpful for studying history. **Historical maps** show things such as where explorers travelled to discover new lands. This helps readers see how difficult their trips might have been.

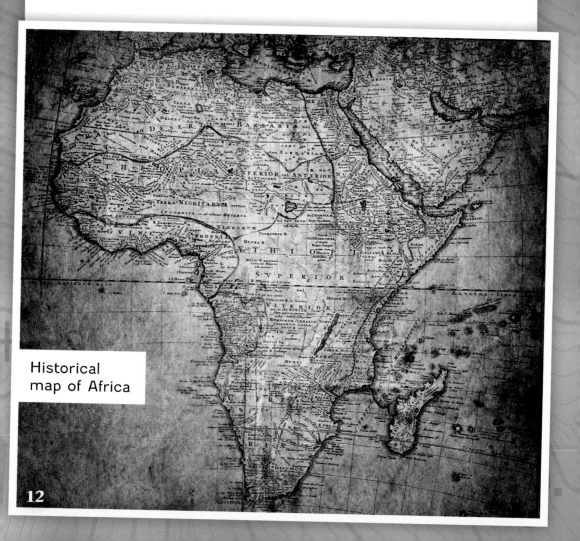

Historical map of Africa

Political maps

Political maps show the size, shape and location of countries around the world. People use political maps to locate their country and other countries. They can also use them to find the county or state they live in.

Countries of Europe

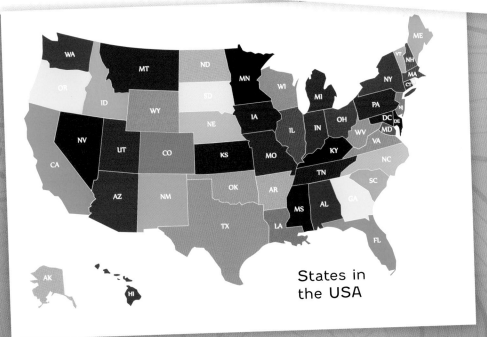

States in the USA

Cities are shown on political maps. People use these maps to find where the capital city is in a country or state. They also read political maps to locate big cities in states or countries.

Road maps

People use road maps to help them plan the best way to travel from one place to another. When planning a short or long trip, road maps can be used to locate streets and major roads in a certain city or county.

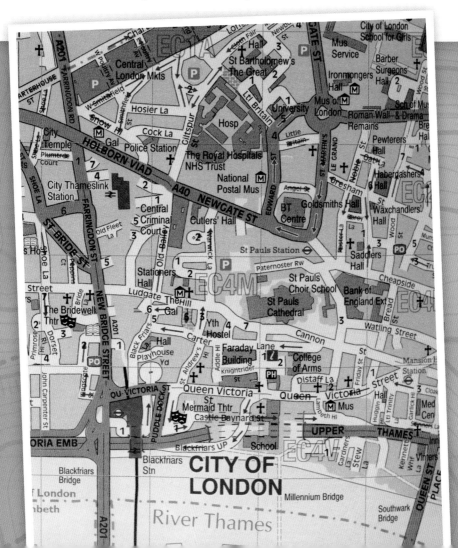

Map features

Mapmakers often need to include a great deal of information in a small space. They use a variety of features to help people quickly find information.

Map title

Maps sometimes have a **map title**. The map title is often written at the top of the map in larger print. The title tells readers what type of map is shown and the area covered by the map.

COUNTRIES OF THE UNITED KINGDOM

Compass rose

Some maps have a **compass rose**. This feature shows where north, south, east and west are on a map. It helps travellers know what direction to take to get to their location. A compass rose also shows where to look on a map when trying to locate a certain place.

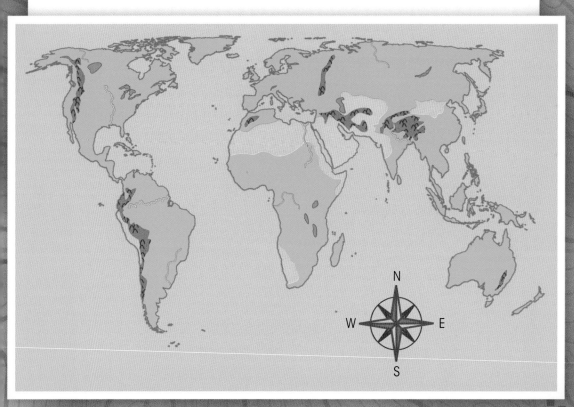

Symbols

Mapmakers use a variety of symbols, or simple pictures or marks. Symbols represent places, such as roads, airports and lakes on a map. For example, the symbol for a mountain could be a triangle. The symbol for an airport could be an aeroplane. Some symbols are a certain colour, such as blue for lakes. Symbols provide the reader with quick ways to locate these places.

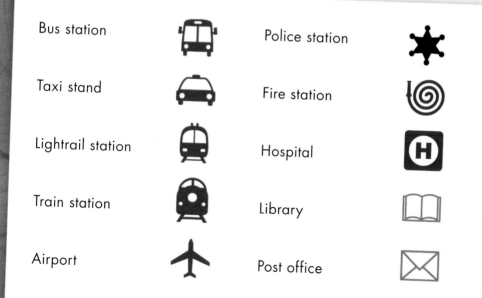

Bus station		Police station	
Taxi stand		Fire station	
Lightrail station		Hospital	
Train station		Library	
Airport		Post office	

These are some of the many symbols found on maps.

Map legend

A **map legend** or **map key** shows the symbols on a map and what each symbol represents. It is often found in a box on the map where it can quickly be read.

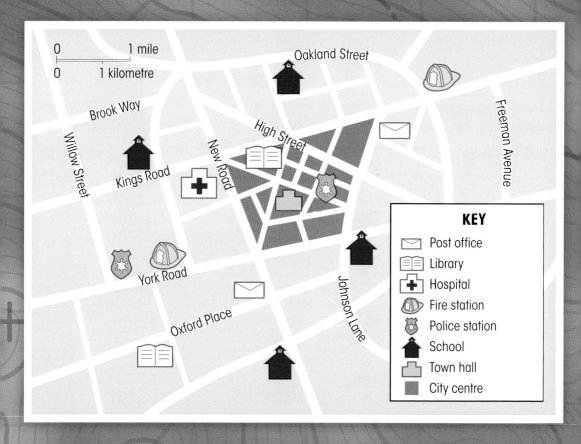

Map scale

People use maps to find out how far away one place is from another. They use the **map scale** to help them do this. This map scale is shown in feet and metres.

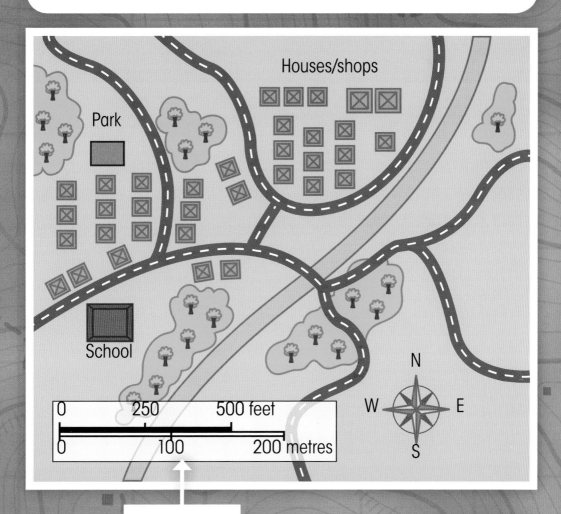

map scale

This map scale shows two symbols that look like rulers. One symbol is marked in kilometres and the other is marked in miles. The scales show how to use the distance measured on the map to determine the distance in kilometres or miles between places in the world.

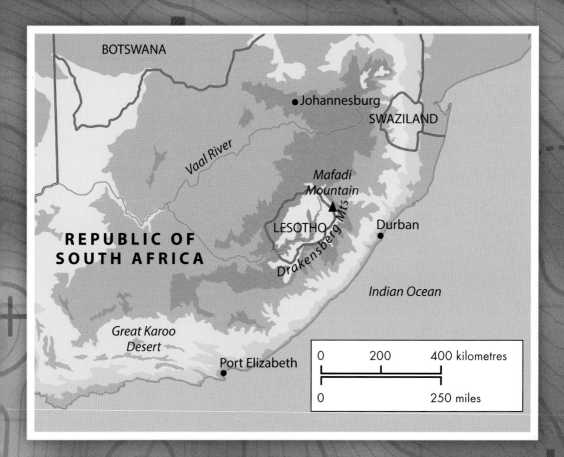

BOTSWANA

• Johannesburg

SWAZILAND

Vaal River

Mafadi Mountain

LESOTHO

Durban

REPUBLIC OF
SOUTH AFRICA

Drakensberg Mts

Indian Ocean

Great Karoo Desert

Port Elizabeth

| 0 | 200 | 400 kilometres |

| 0 | | 250 miles |

Labels

Mapmakers use labels to identify or name places on a map. Countries, cities and towns are labelled. Oceans, landforms and regions are labelled. Roads, bridges and parks are also labelled.

Map lines

Some maps have lines on them. These lines help people to read maps quickly. They also divide Earth into different parts.

Latitude and longitude

Mapmakers sometimes draw **latitude** and **longitude** lines on maps. Latitude lines are drawn around the Earth from west to east. Longitude lines are drawn around the Earth from north to south. All longitude lines go through the North Pole and South Pole.

Latitude and longitude lines can be used to help people locate a certain place on a map.

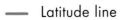

—— Latitude line

——— Longitude line

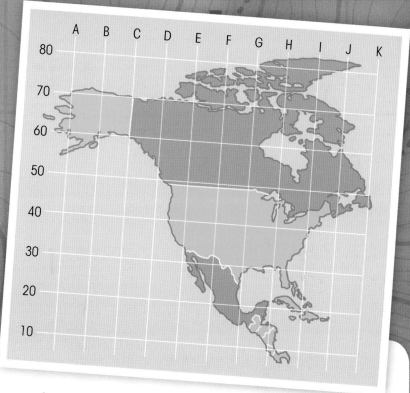

Using a grid system

The latitude lines on a map go from left to right. The longitude lines go up and down. When latitude and longitude lines cross each other, they make a **grid**. They form areas that look like squares.

Sometimes mapmakers label the squares with a letter and a number. They then make a list of places on the map, with a letter and number written next to them.

The letter and number tell you where to look on the map to find each place. For example, on the map below the shopping centre is listed as B3.

By finding square B and then moving up to square 3, you will find where the shopping centre is located.

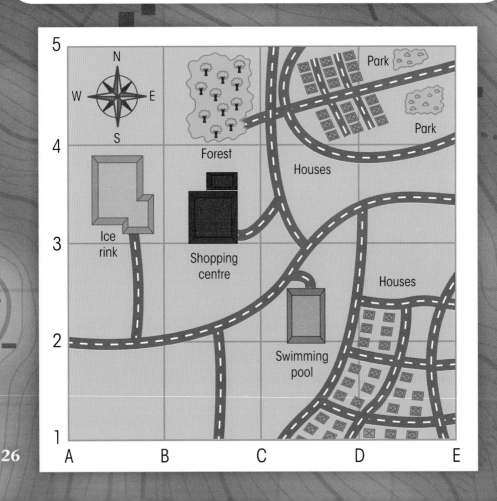

Equator

The **equator** is the latitude line that is located midway between the North Pole and the South Pole. It divides the Earth into the two parts known as the Northern **Hemisphere** and the Southern Hemisphere.

Prime meridian

The **prime meridian** is the longitude line that goes through an area called Greenwich in London. This line also divides the Earth into the two parts known as the Western Hemisphere and the Eastern Hemisphere.

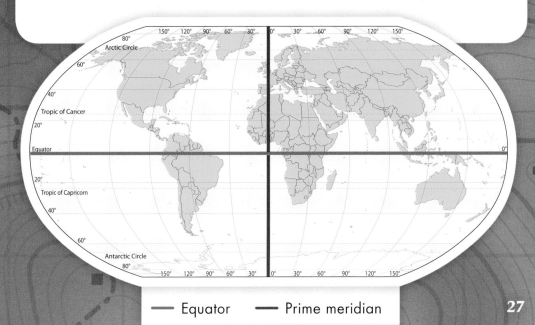

—— Equator ▬▬ Prime meridian

New maps

The size and shape of landforms around the world have changed over time. Sometimes new lakes or rivers are formed or older ones change. New physical maps are made to show these changes.

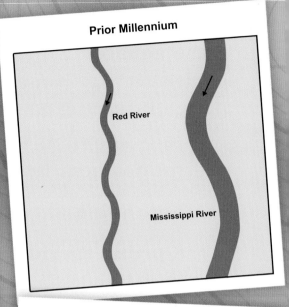

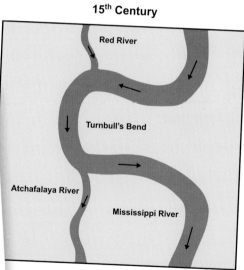

Maps showing how a river changed over time

Sometimes a country's borders are changed. For example, it may become bigger or smaller. New countries or cities are formed. When this happens, new political maps are drawn to show these changes.

Czechoslovakia before 1993

The area became two countries in 1993.

Why maps are important

Maps are important for many reasons. They help us see how the Earth looks and how its land, water and climates are changing over time. The borders and names of countries and cities have changed and will most likely continue to change. Maps help us see these changes.

Finally, as people travel more and more, they will continue to rely on maps to help them find their way. Maps help us understand the world in which we live.

Glossary

climate map shows the temperature, rainfall or snowfall in an area during a particular time period

compass rose shows where north, south, east and west are on a map

equator imaginary latitude line that goes around the centre of the Earth

grid imaginary areas on a map that look like squares

hemisphere on a map, this represents one half of a globe or the Earth

historical map shows important information about the past

latitude lines drawn around the Earth from west to east; they are imaginary lines

location exact place where something is

longitude lines drawn around the Earth from north to south, which all go through the North Pole and the South Pole; they are imaginary lines

map legend or **map key** feature that shows what symbols are found on a map and what they represent

map scale tells you how to determine the distance from one location to another on a map

map title tells you the area covered by the map and the type of map

physical map shows continents, oceans, landforms and waterways

political map shows countries, counties and cities

prime meridian imaginary longitude line that goes through Greenwich in London

road map shows roads and motorways for an area, such as a county or city

Index